Bann Al-Sukhni is a poet. She also enjoys writing children's stories and is the author of *I'd Rather Be Me*, a children's book. *Recalling Nirvana* is Bann's first poetry collection. She lives in Ontario, Canada.

Bann Al-Sukhni

RECALLING NIRVANA

AUSTIN MACAULEY PUBLISHERS™

LONDON · CAMBRIDGE · NEW YORK · SHARJAH

Ordering Information:
Quantity sales: special discounts are available on quantity purchases by corporations, associations, and others. For details, contact the publisher at the address below.

Publisher's Cataloguing-in-Publication data
Al-Sukhni, Bann
Recalling Nirvana

ISBN 9781643788944 (Paperback)
ISBN 9781643788197 (Hardback)
ISBN 9781645755869 (ePub e-book)

Library of Congress Control Number: 2020902907

www.austinmacauley.com/us

First Published (2020)
Austin Macauley Publishers LLC
40 Wall Street, 28th Floor
New York, NY 10005
USA

mail-usa@austinmacauley.com
+1 (646) 5125767

Table of Contents

I Promise You

I promise you
Your love did not go to waste
Because of you I lived a different life
And while I can't say
I know anything about
How you stayed sane
In a world of fakes
Or the way you chose to navigate that internal maze
Or even your true fate
I know I love you
I'm not afraid to state how I feel
In regard to your story
Told by those who claim to be on your team
They say you were so great
That your efforts kept our faith safe
To this day
But their stories lack taste
They strip you of your worth
Speaking only of sacrifice and pain
You became a generic persona
And I find it hard to relate
But I still stand for you
Because I know you'd stand for me
Because everything you fought for is at stake
Those stories they tell don't speak your truth
I read between the lines
And my love for you grew
Which wasn't a choice
And will only increase
But are you proud?
Or has my love gone to waste

I Lose Myself

You'll find my roots
In incomparable territory
In the toughest climate
I've grown
Sporting the most delicious fruit
Until a humbling disaster
Forces a final goodbye
To all I've come to know
To my outstretched branches
And erect pride
All feels lost
But a lyrical force
Soon sings to me
About a land of freedom
And opportunity
Slightly hardened, yet intact
My seed takes flight
And for a quarter of a century, I lose myself
In smoke
Fog
And
Piercing melodies
Until I settle
In another home
On another land
Brilliantly, on my own
Just west of painful memories

Frozen in Time

Last November
You mentioned a land
That was dear to your heart
It seemed so grand

When I questioned you further
You explained it to me
It was where you grew up
And you wanted me to see

So we got in your car
I needed to know
More about the place
That made you so

We drove and drove
Past the loveliest trees
Hours must have passed
Yet time seemed to freeze

I didn't see it coming
But you changed everything
When you pulled the car over
And took out a ring

Now every single night
'Fore I go to sleep
I whisper your name
Your memory I keep

The Finish Line

I have dreams, I have hopes
I have things I want
I have worries, I have fears
Sometimes I'll complain
I pray to God
Things go my way
I pray for others too
But
Truth is
I have one goal
For me to make it through
To make it 'cross
The finish line
Don't matter if I'm bruised
Don't care if I
Finish last
Or if I can't find you
Just want to cross the finish line
Just want to make it through

Read This Book

Read this book so you may learn to be less passionate
Too much passion leads you down the wrong path
The path you seek requires just the right amount of passion

Open this book and read its words, without guilt and without emotional investment

Open this book and read its words for what they are: information, data, ideas

Only then will you be directed down the path you seek

Before you open this book, drop the dogma; being closed-minded will make your mind useless to everything this masterpiece has to offer

If you feel you make most of your decisions out of fear, open this book

Oasis

You are my greatest escape
My soul's oasis
My pillow, when I need to rest my head for just a few seconds
My door to possibilities of which I've only dreamed
My shadow's unconditional love

The Ring

Whips, words
Scars
In spite of it all, she's gotten so far
When it gets too much, she goes to the ring
Sweats, swings
Relieves tension
Breathes again
And it's back to routine
Kids, husband, parents, work
For which she's ever so grateful
But sometimes when she feels like she's being ambushed
She takes a moment
Then heads to the ring
His face on her mind, she throws a punch
She doesn't stop until she's breathing hard
She'll make it because she takes care
Though she puts others first
To herself she's fair
Though he caused so much pain
Her will is strong
And her heart is rare
And when she needs it
The ring is there

Company

The best company comes from making it through the worst times alone
You're stronger
Don't need others like you did before
You give new meaning to the word independent
And in addition to bringing your own nonsense to the table
You also share your own wisdom
And it should be noted that company tempers you
Keeps your mind fresh
With ideas that are hard to sit with
So you are always on your feet
Don't be afraid of being alone
You'll find good company soon enough
And good news
You can be your own person
Because while you may be what you eat
You are not the company you keep

Chords

You haven't asked, but I know you wonder
Well, let me make it more clear
I do love you deeply
I want to feel your arms around me
Because a touch of your body is sweeter than a sugar rush
I want to get my fill of you
Because a glance into those eyes makes me lost in the depths of your strength
I want to hear your voice
Because I trust those chords
More than the ones in any piece of music
It's clear why I love you so
But I've told you before
Why you love me
Is something I just don't know
The only thing I want
Is to do right by you
To be your muse
When you crave inspiration
To join you on the journey of life
To stand by your side
Whatever the cause
Because your instincts are right
Your soul a true guide
And your heart
The best flashlight

Smart Play

Your next play will be smart
So beautiful, like art
Something to think about
And make you gain perspective
When perspective does not come easy
The secret to a smart play
Is in fact balance
To take the middle path
Which sounds simpler than it is
Knowing the middle road requires seeing the extremes for what they are
Which is a difficult task if these extremes are examined one at a time
For extremes are indeed relative
So smart plays also require quick thinking and multitasking
And you are the quickest thinker around
You play your hand before others realize you've drawn
And we all know multitasking is your default
Explaining the game for those who are lost
While putting everyone else to shame
With an incredibly smart play

The Light

The tree leans towards the sun
We do the same
When it comes to light
While the tree sits quietly in the dark
We complain
But if we reflect
It is pointless to place blame
That's the devil's game
No
Live this life for what it is
Paradise
Want God to approve?
Roll the dice
Make your move
And be grateful that you were given a choice
And when you come upon the illusion of strife
Instead of putting up a fight
Just lean
Lean towards the light

Ship at Sea

I am a ship at sea
Built to go the distance
In submission to the elements
Able to make it
Through the toughest storms
Endowed with the task
Of getting us to shore

I am a ship at sea
At times I am lost
Calm in the day
And in the night
My form an outline
Against a proud sky
Whose sun and moon light up my path
I give hope
To the lost I come across
And as I take them
To solid ground
I realize
I am found

Brilliant

You, who was swept away by the beckoning breeze
You, who loved your home, but took leave
You, who gave up riches to be able to see
Do not fear
There is safety
Stability
Serenity
Written in future hours
Let them pass
Over the wall you built with your broken heart
Let them bring it down, brick by brick
Do not search for peace
Let it find you
Do this
And you'll find trust too
So even if you are uprooted a thousand times over
You will get through it
You will be better than before
And when you walk through that door
You will dazzle all with your glow
And you will be grateful for the breeze
Which made you resilient
And brought you to this place
Where you could be brilliant

All the Birds

All the birds
In the world
Said you had been untrue
I said they were mistaken
I kept my faith in you
'Cause I believe
My voice still means
Something to your ears
That your heart still
Races fast
Whenever I am near
I know you care
In you I trust
I know your love is true
But the songs these birds keep singing
Have got me feeling blue

A Changed Man

I glance out my window
And I see the man I know
I don't always catch him
But I never miss his glow
His singing wakes me up
Though I'm not asleep
His gentle movements
Make my heart leap
I think back to when
We'd walk side by side
While I would be worried
He took things in stride
Now he is his image
I get what I see
No need for symbolism
Dear bird, you are free

A Dream

Dream big
You cannot lose
Dream of love, peace and seeking truth
Though it may scare you
Dream of change
Make that your goal, make that your aim
Though you may pray
For smoother days
Your heart, it craves
To be saved
It wants a say
For its owner's sake
Heed its wisdom
'Cause you truly need
The bumps in the road
The dead ends in the street
For you will conquer
Fear of losing your blessings
And you will be stronger
As you choose new directions
Your heart, it knows
To be saved
You must find
That you are brave
And all it takes
Is a dream
A dream for choice
A dream of change

Magpie

Oh, magpie
While I guarantee
That you know what you need
You'll never be happy
Until you get what's shiny

Dear God-Appointed Guardians

Dear God-appointed guardians
You've been there through it all
More recently
When it got a little too much
But also way back
When I first started to crawl
When I took my first steps
Learning to walk
And I'm sure we have a photo of that somewhere
You were always there
Cheering me on
A chorus of "Banns"
Making me so strong
Protecting my heart
So that I could get here
And while here is not always pretty
I'm ready
And I'm blessed with that knowledge
Because I had you then
And I have you now
You still love me
Taking pride in my light
And standing by my shadow
Though it follows me wherever I go
It took me too long
But I finally see
You're not just family
You're lifesavers
And God will reward you

This I don't doubt
Just hope He'll ask me
To carry it out

Courage

When I look back
My faith increases
And I'm no longer scared
I remember His favor upon me
All the blessings
And how I always found solace in prayer
I know the path I've chosen
Isn't at all easy
But I've finally found the truth
And I'm not sorry
I prayed for salvation
And I always felt so close
Yet at the same time
I couldn't claim it
So now that I walk this path
I feel at peace
I know God has forgiven
Those sins I cannot bear
I finally mean it when I say
I'm His
My life
Is for Him, I swear
Though I don't feel like a martyr
As I make sure to remember
The words He says with care
With every difficulty comes ease
With every difficulty comes ease
These words take away the fear
I take a look back
My faith increases
Courage, I proudly wear

The Best Is Yet to Come

Let us look forward
Upon an ocean of our future
Each creature within it
Remains to be seen
Until we dive down
To a place of which we dreamed
Where Time is the best guide
To be in harmony
With these humbling creatures
Designed to live for moments
In the most peaceful of waters
In such a kingdom
Of promised revelations
The best is yet to come

Mind

Right direction
Stars align
Shower of blessings
Life is kind
So why, oh, why
Can't I unwind?
A crash course in Mind
Leads me to find
That I can write
My blessed life
So what do I do?
I write out the strife
And without a second glance
I leave behind
These blinding signs

Remission

I live with my sins
Piercing holes in this ship
Once carefree and floating
Now in weaker moments
For years I've feared
Losing to these waters
I made a promise though
To find a patch of hope
And salvage this ship
Though it may seem
Too broken to fix
But I will
By all that is holy, I will
Direct this vessel
To a land of permission
Explicit remission
Where sacred healing
Can finally begin
Until then, though
I live with my sins

Shot in the Dark

I go running
From dusk until dawn
I crave the escape
Since you've been gone

It doesn't make sense
The way I feel now
We'd always fight
When you were around

I feel such sadness
And deep regret
But the tears haven't come
As of yet

I tell myself
When I'm feeling low
That faith will get me through this
It's all that I know

I just want your forgiveness
Though I know I have it
I was wrong all along
And that makes me sick

Mama, I'm sorry
I just did what I knew
Please pray for me
God knows I pray for you

Trains

Corrupt conversations
In a smoke-filled station
Are at once broken
When a voice, truly foreign
Makes a startling claim
Some trains
Have been proven unsafe
At this announcement
Some people try to escape
But they do this in vain
Security is ready for this day
As for those who are relieved
Their lives have been saved
They know which train they'll take

Invalid

Your thoughts are invalid
Your statements don't hold
They're noise in the background
They don't have me sold

You say that I listen
In fact I just hear
To another you glisten
He lends you his ear

You're bold and you know it
But courage, you lack
With knives up your sleeves
You strike from the back

You're sure that I'm losing
On weak hearts you've preyed
Of my strength you're clueless
I won't be your aid

You think you're a burden
But you're welcome to stay
I'm playing, not fighting
That's all I will say

Crossing Borders

Crossing borders
To an unknown space
Where fixed fear
Is a saving grace
A simple tool
To navigate
A war-torn land
A corrupt state
But, still
Sweet home awaits
Where bold hearts
Are embraced
And as promised
All fear, erased

Riches

Don't miss it
In just seconds
A shooting star
Can grant you riches
You'd ask for love
And you'd get your wish
Though it should be noted
In your interest
The love you seek
Is holographic
To find yourself
Is the best request

Joy Ride

Joy ride—
And I'm alive
Almost convinced
This feeling won't die
But I've been through this
Too many times
So while I might
Err on caution's side
I'd rather drive
For miles and miles
Because I know
When I'm too tired
And I can barely see my lights
I'll think back to this time
And I'll cruise by

Divinity

The enemy in sight
A stunning one indeed
For you are almost blinded by fear
Yet even more marvelous
Is what you don't see
You're sure you fight alone
But I spot an army
Your instincts make you frightened
But respond calmly
Because the view from up top
Shows Divinity

She's Painted Blue

She's painted blue
The artists would do
Anything to prove
Their story was true
But fiction
Is easily brewed
A tempting concoction
For a foolish few
Who would down this drink
And proceed to drive
A world-altering tale
Into the fragile hearts
And weaker minds
Of those without a clue
But God have mercy
On a mistaken group
Who lived its life
By what it knew
That this woman was in mourning
That this woman was blue

Chance Reaction

A chance reaction
Leaves me in your orbit
But I worry about the space between us
So you hold onto me
Won't let me go
Though passing Adams
Try to get close
Though I lack positivity
You see past it all
You know what I can be
You're confident I can lead
A life of meaning
Our bonds are a relief
For thirsty hearts
No need for fear
Our chemistry is clear

Moments Away

Struggling
In the deep end
Of inconsistent waters
Seeking to find a calm
Long enough to do ablutions
No matter how much I fight it
I seem to only sink deeper
Alternating between gasps for air
And gulps of another life force
I realize to work this system
To which I am inextricably bound
I must let go
After all, the splashing
Which is worsening the panic
Of this weary swimmer
Is also unnecessary
The guards are merely moments away

Numbers

The door is in front of you
Leave at any time
Guess the numbers lying
In the mad king's mind
And the lock will click open
But at this rate
Your last breath will be
In this suffocating space
You need assistance and you can't ask for hints
For the king is a special one indeed
He cannot be seen
You've tried countless combinations
Now you're praying for help
Begging, praising the king
You pray for patience, to be well
But what you pray most for is
To know the king's mind
You swear this is all you'll ever need
But please, spare yourself the worry
You are the most creative addition
To a generation of gentler servants
Your moves are calculated
And everyone around you
Tries to do the math
To see just what you're seeing
But their numbers are off
They could never imagine your guiding dilemma
You want everyone to be top-grade without you being anything less than the best
Still, you would give up rarity for another soul's peace
Think on it not a moment longer

Your hopes for others will be realized
But not at the expense of your desire to be different
You see
Your perspective is yours alone
It will set you free
And while you feel you have been burdened by bad luck
I urge you to take a look past your supplicating hands
You'll find something you recognize instantly
The key to the damned door sits at your feet, where it always sat
Waiting to be seen
You were never meant to know the king's digits
Your perspective is all you need

Secrets

I crave Your embrace
You're my closest confidant
You keep all my secrets safe
But I feel drained
I don't feel You as I'd like to
And You say
You're closer to me than my vein
But right now, I feel alone
How much
Only You'd know
I swear
I want to grow
But I feel weak
Incapable of change
I'd love to abstain
From repeated mistakes
But that possibility feels
So far away
Take away this buried shame
And with it, the endless pain
That resurfaces every day
Even though I tell myself
It's fine, life's okay
I'll make it through
How can I feel alone
I have You

The Constant

A closer look reveals a ticker tape
Whose bold messages flash at only your eyes
You're confused and flattered at the same time
You're tired of seeing your name
All day, and all night
But it's always been there, this ticker tape
It'll always be there
The one constant in your life
But look at the bright side
While you're no longer always right
You're also no longer blind
You have what you need to fight
Because despite what the ticker tape insists
There is a war going on
And though the ticker tape functions to prove that it has value
It has none
A powerful system created by a clever bunch
So while your ticker tape makes you unique
It is irrelevant to the choices you make
The worst thing that can happen is for you to get flustered and lose your way
Don't be fooled, live your life
Let the ticker tape roll by

After-Taste

Half-empty
And my poison has left you the same
You may want to blame me
But you let yourself break
You went insane
And right away
You craved my warm embrace
You'll regret me in the morning
But for now, it's no mistake
I'm still on your lips, surrender's on your face
Who knew this is how hell would taste?
But you won't accept this fate
You'll do whatever it takes
To get out of this mess
That wasn't entirely yours
And when all else fails
You'll pray
Because you believe you can be saved
And you know your heart
It only wants to help
Yet you're still looking to me
With self-doubt in your eyes
Well, don't be surprised
I've only ever offered you
A distorted view of life

Sacred as Sin

Which brings one closer to God
And leaves one unafraid of death
Eager for face-to-face forgiveness

Tree Leaves

Tree leaves
Green, brown and red
In the fall
Make me want to walk
To the nearest lake
Sparkling blue
Makes me want to write
About God, life and us
The words on these pages
Deep, and full of youth
Make me miss you

Time

A sun to a blue sky
A moon inspiring ocean tides
A star in the blackest night
The calm in a cosmic fight
And after all is said and done
A moment in time

The Royals

My last breath will be loyal
Unregretful
Wise
I won't be scared
Not with you by my side
And them waiting to greet me
Once I close my eyes
My last breath will be right
No mistakes
No worries
About leaving this life behind
Or finding something I won't like
On the other side
I will be excited
But calm
Beyond ready
To finally move on
My last breath will be perfect
But until then
I live in this moment
Neither rushing my breaths
Nor afraid of promised death
Concerned only of staying true
So when it's time to meet the royals
I'll know my last breath was loyal

The Stars

You're halfway across the world
As far as I'm concerned
Your glow lingers though
In the stars we used to gaze at
Too many years ago
On that porch of yours
The last time I saw you
We spent the night
Under the stars
Laughing
Because you have the most refreshing sense of humor
And you know just what makes me smile
That night you promised you'd never leave me
So you can understand these tears I cry
You can appreciate these red eyes
I don't know where you are
But I miss riding in your car
How you'd sound on your guitar
How I'd make you pose for my art
How you'd kiss me before we'd part
How you'd listen to my beating heart
I promised something too
That I'd fight as I always do
So three years later I still fight
And it helps to gaze at the stars at night

A Message to My Superhero

I almost let go
You took my hand once more
But really all I needed was to let go

I almost fell
You caught me
But really all I wanted was to fall all the way

This life almost blew me away
You chained my cape to the ground
But how was I supposed to fly?

I can let go
Fall
Be blown away at any time
And survive

I am a superhero too
I just never knew it with you

The Lights

But the lights have been dimmed
We're dancing in puddles of sin
We search not for a rope
Though there are rumors
That we may sink
Indeed, we fall
But it is all in fun
We are soon up again
No, we know who we belong to
But who will you turn to when you fall into the hole
That you spoke of
And that filled your thoughts?

Walls

At birth, I saw walls
Icy blue
But you were home
And I was warm

Still young
I was sure I saw right through you
So I opened up
Hoping you'd do the same

Now I am old, and I stare at walls
Grateful that no one knows their tongue

I Accept

Sorrow had etched its mark
On her unrelenting heart
That delivered boldly and blindly
To a body in debt
But when she was forced to flee
Faith appeared once more
Smiling peacefully
In green and gold
At this sight, she remembered
How God opens doors
And with complete trust, she said
I accept

Falls

These falls are a release
For jaded eyes
A shower of blessings
Free of disguise
Eroding pride
Highlighting fragile life
Upon careful reflection
A wronged heart
Races right
To these falls
Grateful
For the All-Wise
A mortal's paradise

Destiny

The universe was written for you and me
Meant solely to guide us to our destiny
We hear every word
And every melody
So together, we dance
Broken lemon seeds at our feet

Colors

All the colors
I've ever seen
Cannot compare
To those I learned as a child
Red, blue, yellow
When I grew older
I learned white
Was all the colors
And life got more complicated

Blue

A push from Yellow Hope
Goodbyes are kept tightly within Pandora's chest
Notorious Yellow
Claims the world as its stage
And hearts as its own
Without your blazing blue
She sits, waiting for hands to make their move
She prays for your return
Let this world be true
She can't live in an amber world
One without you
But there's a rumor that you make glasses
That grant the owner perspective
Lend her a pair
She can't afford to lose her vision

Caution

Oh, friend
I sit for hours by you
Negotiating common ground
Our debates making all of this village
Peek out stained-glass windows
Quench this tongue, which has grown thirsty from denying death
Take these shoes which can only get me so far
I trust you will, for who will, if not you
Teach me how to ride these waves
Before my tongue and feet
No longer heed caution

Lifeline

Lengths, widths, moments that were measured
We spent ages gazing at the stars each night
Each night I saw him in my mind
Each leg a lifeline
Four eyes, all true
The strangest sight!
I couldn't move
Frozen in space
Mocked by time
I was counting
The seconds before
What I was sure
Would unfold
But fate would not see my end
By treacherous web
No, I lived
I lived
And with a little patience
His cravings would dissipate
Win-win

Power

Take my hand
I'll take you further
You wanted forgiveness
I'll show you power

The kind that makes most mad
But it won't change you
Though you will find yourself
Running to truth

I'll give you a chance
To make a change
When you take it
You'll feel old scars fade

I don't deserve this
You'll say, eyes dazed
But I'll see right through them
You're so much stronger than you claim

And you'll find it funny
Because you knew all along
That you were my enemy
And I, your favorite song

Freedom: Part I

God, I feel so free
You, who finally completed
Years of fatigue-inducing study
For the prestige
Would be jealous of me
That bird you watch when you're tired of reading over-priced textbooks
Which has just learned to fly
Sees me
And doesn't know how to feel
Yes, this freedom
I was missing
Is finally here
And as with all things
Freedom cannot be found directly
If you tried to locate my freedom
To try to steal it from me
You'd find it an impossible task
Because even if you invented the right instrument
To do just that
You would see where my freedom was last
Where it took me
But you won't ever find it
Or me for that matter
Because there's knowledge you lack
You can't find me
I could be standing right in front of you
And you would be clueless as to where I am
Because you have no idea who I am
And if you don't know a subject's properties
You won't know what you're looking at
I used to worry

I used to fret
That you would never accept the real me
Because I know you
And you only see what you want to see
But in reality
Your vision is 20/20
Your concern, I'll diagnose
Pathological hypocrisy
You say you care about me
You speak of goodness
Opportunities for all
A life of ease
But when I wanted to play
Join this sweet game of which you speak
You said I must pay a cost
When I asked, I learned
The cost is me
And I knew
No tears
No fear
My thoughts were confirmed
I am an island
That the universe wants to own
But soon everyone will know
While I was an oasis for the world before
My trees providing serene shade
My waters a sight for sore eyes
My fruit the most satisfying fuel
I will not be used
Though you've created a storm
To try to bring down my trees
And ravage my beauty
My island is in your eye
It always will be
So while it's only me that you see
I have my sights set on fulfilling my destiny
I thought you were my curse
But as my greatest test
You were also my greatest mercy

I know who I am now
I know my worth
And damn
I'm free

Truth

Truth will not be said
Not if it must be stated
It sits in the greedy stomachs
Of those who have not waited
Of those who refuse patience
Of those who share fables
With smiling faces
Truth is oppressed
Waiting for a savior
That was my only prayer
But when I regurgitated speech
I saw what I said
And patience I bled

Stability

Could you be a candidate?
Take the test
All you need
Is honesty
To stop going in circles

First, you must see
Who makes the decisions here?
If you say, me
Do you persevere?
In which way?
You're human, it seems
So how many casualties
Before things are clear?

Will you stand up with a plan
When it's time to speak?
Or lie on the couch
With a dry mouth
Playing it by ear?

So far
Have you fibbed, even a bit?
If so, go right back
To where you did

For the rest
Who have done their best
When it is said
That things happen for a reason
Do you nod your head?

Is this statement
True, false, or irrelevant?

If you were so close
Then at last gained the throne
To a kingdom
And a key to all of its doors
With a castle so vast
And skilled servants to ensure
Your needs are all met
Without one word
But there was a choice
To let go of it all
Do you know if you could?
Or have I made your blood boil?
Without a kingdom or key in hand

Now, to reflect
On the internal show
That plays each night
And breaks your flow
Are you at peace
With your bold shadow?
Or do you deny it
Try to hide it
Does it still cause you sorrow?

Many questions asked
Yet another this test lacks
When your greatest challenge in life
Finally arrives
Will you turn to another
Or trust your own mind?

Self-Intercession

Do I please
The one whom I want to please
Or am I stuck
In a rut
Lost at sea

Oh, God
You've given me a choice
To do right by You
As to what makes You happy
I think I've got a clue

But it's simply not something
People would believe
My heart is Yours I swear
Courage I proudly wear
But when it comes to You
This load is hard to bear
Even if You whispered in my ear
That You were happy with me
I would not be satisfied
This I guarantee

I do it for You and for me
Because I cannot stand the thought
Of losing You, oh God
Of losing myself

I stand in front of You
After making ablutions
And I ask, as I always will

For strength and confidence
Oh God, I'm Yours
You know my heart
But I'm surrounded by people
Who would love to tear me apart

And they would say I sin
But they're filled with hate
Your messenger taught us
To live in a loving state

Dear God, once more
I know, I'm for You
But should I believe what they say
Or are you mine, too?

Kindness

An ode to no harm
But we are in a desert
I ask for a chance
Let us dance this dance
Of feverish mistakes
Until we land on the path
Of truth content
The only one that never fades
For we have the will
And we know the way
Though it's not enough to say
A thing
It's never enough to pray it to be true
Without conviction
Without knowledge
We'll always have distorted views
And every act we take in this stage
Will guide us to another mirage
And we will tell ourselves
Mirages are beautiful
Glory be to God
Because clearly
This was meant to be
To see this water
For moments
Only to face reality
Where else could you find
Such symbolic beauty
But I don't think any of us
Really want to stay the same

So perhaps this is also
An ode to change

Lucky

We're hungry
And we always get what we need
I'm lucky
Because I need to be
Somewhere I do not know
Beyond imagination
A place that causes fascination
And now I'm glowing
From anticipation
I see opportunities
Just out of reach
Manifesting magically in my life
And so I learn
If I think it, it can come to be
But there's also hidden fruit
In the Knowledge Tree

Happy

To see beauty, and to feel its pull
To do right by God, to feel full
To honor truth when news seems urgent
To be of the few who are honored servants
To find the old has started to crack
Due not to age, but to a bad back
That's not to say
That all were blind
Maybe the songs they sang
Never played in their mind
Maybe they knew what
We never will
Or maybe we could know
Though we would have to rush down
This hill
And to climb to the top once again
Would take just seconds
But for those whose thoughts
Are more sacred to them
Than God's love
A dilemma ensues
Continue to hum, or stay true
And we all know what they will choose
God's love is forgotten
But those songs have
A special place in their heart
Those who claim they love
By the old
Are truly bold
They think and assume they know
But they know not

They think, and they are lost
They think their elevation
Means they are at the top
But this is nothing new
And I will no longer fret
For those without a clue

Patient

You hold honesty above patience
But you are honestly mistaken
If you cannot wait, you cannot choose
And that's why the impatient lose
When I say
Take a moment, hesitate
You're sure this means I've gone astray
But I am certain it is brave
A certainty that slowly came
When all my stars aligned
Stars that cannot be read
Part of a solar system that cries
Out in my defense
One that relies
On a universe, patient
Perpetually in prostration
To revealing rhythm and tasteful time

Irrelevance

The sweetest perspective
A benign acceptance

Fearless

I just hope
You know something I don't
All these moves
I've taken to get close
Have left me fearless
I say fearless, not brave
Because I mean what I say
I do not aim
To manipulate
Which I agree
Is something anyone can state
Be it an act of truth
Or one of shame
But perhaps you will judge me
On my intentions
For those are all I can claim
My actions are simply responses
But my soul initiates
An outstanding argument
For the sake of tolerance
I've realized I've coped all along
To the rhythm in a song
That, by mercy, does not end
And they say
The soul cannot argue for itself
On judgement day
Well, if I may say so
I'd like to make my case
Before I know my fate
I may be fearless
But I want to be brave

And this is the only way
So I just hope
You know something I don't

The Butterfly

What a shame
I've been bought
Though I fought it
I don't quite mind
How I look through this frame
I can't wait
For you to know me
And the time will come
For you to let go

Time will pass
Just as my life did
But its stages continue
To remain intriguing
Arousing seemingly illogical sentiment
When it was a life like any other
But people crave royalty
Like I craved change

Time would stand
When what needed transformation
Gives way to imitation
Dreamt up at conception
Never abandoned
Yet, when plans began to fray
I waited
Resisting breakage
And at once
Made a sophisticated
Kind of statement
Still

All my faces were a reminder
Before my wings ever took me higher

The Fire

I'm not crying about you
I'm crying because I knew
I've known all along
That there was reality
Light
In the direst of plights
But I still can't see it
Why can't I see it?
What's wrong with my sight?
A rare type of blindness
For I can see
But I can't sense light
For those who doubt
There is eternal fire
I can feel it now
But it's a lost fight
I fashioned the fire
With a right mind

Anticipation

For moments that are written sparingly
For glory
That takes its time
Making a brief appearance at the end
With contract in hand
Please note that all memories
Collected on the journey
Will be removed
They are tainted with angst
And can no longer be used
To further the plan
A single choice remains
Give them up
Or be left with chance

Freedom: Part II

I know this to be true
Life imitates art
Which I find rather strange
For Art does not know its nature
It is classified as art
By Life
I know I'm right
But it's not something I can prove
Yet I'm changing
The impulse to know is faltering
Is this way of thinking
Hindering my progression?
Or is it nudging me
Slowly
In a desirable direction?
I push through one-directional trains of thought
For they will not be of use
Incapable of arriving at any destination
Trains of consideration
As I call them
Proudly claim to take into account
Your heart
Mind
And body
But they cannot crack
The vessel wall
Beyond which is the location
I hope
To crack the code
To know the message
Carved within the vessel

I have a destination that I plan on reaching
I will get there
And I'll remind myself along the way
That the place of fascination
Will in fact be
Crucial to the journey
And I will see myself for the first time
As more than a work of art
Greater than a creation
Beyond human classification
Life will be waiting
Evolved, and with open hands
I'll smile
For in one hand will be a file
Indicating every time I made a right
When I could have stopped
In the other, a message from you
I'll choose
Freedom begets truth

Sugar

White capsules, once blue
Sugar pills, through and through
Placebos, to test the glue
That sticks highs to lows, if you only knew
Placebos, another name or hue
Are sugar, if you only knew

Unspoken

Your truest words were unspoken
Kept within your gentle soul
But if we pay attention
We see the way you roll

You loved and you lost
But you were so strong
You focused on the needy
You avoided all wrong

Yet that's not what I see
When I think of you
I see somebody real
So incredibly true

Always doing right
Wasn't on your mind
That's how they tell it
But people can be blind

You simply lived your truth
You learned bit by bit
You were human too
For your faith, the best fit

Privacy

Heaven looks down on me
Its angels smiling gracefully
They see a young lady
Who performs all of her duties

What they do not see
Is what they cannot know
People
Whose nature begs of them to judge
Form their own beliefs
But I don't hold a grudge

You see
I'm quite relieved

I seek to please God
And He grants me humility
The thing that I pray for
Ever so desperately

Heaven watches over me
But even it's not privy
To my whole picture, my full story
Does not know every struggle
Does not see each victory

One more thing to thank God for
Precious privacy

Epic Feminist

The ultimate display of beauty, power, and confidence
She stands for love and independence
The rest is irrelevant
She stops for no one
She lets nothing bring her down
So when the love of her life leaves town
Without warning
Instead of falling apart, she peers into her heart
Forgives
And uses her creativity
To heal
For she realizes that it would be a waste to think anything other than positive
thoughts for herself, her future, and the man that could never hurt her

The Snake

Unravelling, all senses heightened
Shedding light, along with skin
Instinctive pushes
Over ground, detailed with scattered prints
Brushing against uncovered calcium and collagen
Revealing signs of blindness
Mistakes conceived, but always fixed
Six feet removed, then refilled
Muted secrets
Unravelling, all senses heightened
Shedding light, along with skin

The Circle

Grey spaces, no corners to count
Varied voices, that rise and fall
Arms of doubt, that play along a wall
A raised flag, at the front of the hall
A drop of arms, an end to talk
Scattered fabric, amidst porcelain dolls
A volcano of cheers, a light house
A closing of doors, a circle of sound

Believer

It's not that I didn't believe
Far from faithless
I believed in truth
But it was a lonely way to be
Walking the path of honesty
And I was ready
To give away the secrets
That made me
Me
But now I see
Now I see
The truth doesn't set you free
And contrary
To your romantic inclinations
Neither does he
Now my faith is truly unique
Because I believe in myself
My good deeds
Self-generated
Positivity
I believe in me

Forever

And suddenly I'm free
Temporarily, of course
Always temporarily

Until I see the next life
Until that mystery is revealed
I accept these walls surrounding me
I know there will be an end to temporarily

At peace I will be
True freedom I will feel
Forever I will see

Humble

To pass, for the best is yet to come
To pass, on the old runner and his run

Sleep

I've walked this path before
A long, broken set of mirrors
A subjective death
A death from which I wake

Labels

Somehow
The title never stays arranged
The ring never remembers its place
The love grows, but the patience fades
Time heals, while we cry for change
And I'll have you just the same
Because I'm brave
Because I stayed
But I never forget to pray
For those who forgot You, for those who forgot praise
God knows, if given the chance
I'd almost take their place
Almost
Give my heart and soul license
To do their best to erase
Another's pain
All of this I say
But are my words fully sane
Or half-crazed?

A Swan in the Water

There's a swan in the beautiful water
The swan sits elegantly
I watch it for hours

There's a swan in the water
One that I can't reach
I want it closer to me

There's a swan in the water
I can make it move, I can make it ruffle its feathers
But I can't quite grasp it

There's a swan in the water
It's driving me mad
The surrounding blue is meaningless

A Change of Heart

My heart has changed
It still loves Life, but attends fewer of her parties
Its preferred method of travel is no longer magic carpet
It knows its self-worth, but is willing to work with the mind
It is beginning to appreciate its fearful inhabitant
My heart has changed

A Certain Traveler's Guide

We are both new to this
But I am the guide
Listen to my humble tantrums
As I hear your gentle rain
Patter on my heart's content
A rich mix of earth and water
I bring you forth from the dark
I've walked this path a dozen times before

String

I'm on a string
Yours to be precise
But what they don't know
Is I tied it myself
Now it's off
Lying on the shelf

Celebration

Excited, for a longer break
Ready, to fight for what's at stake
Willing, to drop everything it takes
Stable, enough to hold the reins

That One

He looked at me and I knew
You looked at him and he smiled
Blue
For his red smiles are reserved for me alone
True
But I never knew it 'til I knew You

Written

Written before time would tell
Assessed and respected before she fell
Permitted at the risk of hell
Assumptions do not suit you well
She decided not to sell
To listen when she hears bells
She'll regret Nirvana, conceptions held
But assumptions do not suit you well

Irrelevant

When you're headed
In the right direction
The signs of truth along the way
Are irrelevant
And you're never taken
No matter how much he loves you
Or how much you love him
You're free, always free

Stone

Oh, lovers of stone
Let the truth be known
Let it wash out your struggles, may you feel it in your bones
May you choose the light
When darkness meets its match
And slowly
Stack by stack
Melt away the pain
You have the power
And you've seen the stains
Break the mirror
That has brought bad luck
And end the curse
Which has sadly stuck
Because you couldn't see it
You couldn't see worth
You couldn't feel the wisdom
You lost it at birth
But now you have it
So make it known
Oh, you, who bow to stone

Ekleipein

And they fear
But they themselves will prove that nothing is worthy of terror
Not even the Absolute
New ethics allows philosophy to be instrumental; just add intention
Numerous battles fought recklessly against the thought
Of extinction
Evolution persists

The Hyena

Close-ups, unseen to the public eye
A chase, reflected in a clear sky
A catch, monstrosity undenied
Scavengers, ravaging what others tried to hide
Mean, stomachs full, laughter high

The Cell

Effortlessly balanced
A symmetrical vision
Pulling before the push
Lighting at the incision
A core grows stronger, quicker
Fearless decisions
Brave beyond belief
Cellular fission

The Clouds

Complements of the heavens
Sacred signs
Framing sets and rises
Requests for breaks, a naked sun
Slow shifts in frame, the director's cut
Unbuffered light, torn curtains
Abandoned rooms, effects untouched

To Sleep

To close your eyes
To leap, without losing sight
To watch what-ifs make their way by
To feel bottled up lows and injected highs
To be tempted by the fire
To choose the light
To keep a promise you thought was a lie
To let be what is not broken
To fight the hardest fight
Each night

The Catalyst

Revealing reactions
The constant in otherwise inelegant transactions
A catalyst by the clock
Facilitating a photosynthesis in broken buds
Scaffolding self-sufficiency in weary weeds
An alternative to the energy of heat

Stand Up

Stand up for yourself
Before you fall for someone else

Remember Me

Two breaths away from normal
One step away from time
Your words were only formal
With reason, yet no rhyme

You left me for the night
I fell ill along the way
You were my sun, forever bright
You disappeared, every ray

I only have one wish now
Remember me as I was then
For God, I could not see how
I could be myself again

Astray

A dance of light
In your tired eyes
Tells a story
Of lows and highs

You started off so eager
Nothing was out of reach
Straight As in elementary
Your teachers beyond speech

What happened over the years
Was tragic in every way
A hardening of your heart
Led you to go astray

This is your point of view
You hope for some advice
You feel you have failed
You're counting off your vices

But with the possibility
That paths are arbitrary
Your patience, in spite of enlightenment
Is the most private of victories

The Wave

Panoramic, the view is clear now
There's a wave
So titanic, I feel myself bow
I'm a slave

A promise of terror and doom
The fear sweeps over me
I need a way out of this room
This is no way to be

I grab a book, I need a hint
I see the oath of God
Surely, God is with the patient
By those words I am awed

I know this to be true
I can watch the wave
I see a different view
I am not a slave

The Idealist

He placed the crown
Slowly on his head
He closed his eyes
Brown, but also red
He tapped her shoulder
Asking what she had read
He turned around
Forgetting all that was said
He looked up
Remembering what he'd promised
He opened his mouth
With hopes he wouldn't fret
He gave his best speech
Written by his best friend

A Feeling

Expressed most potently in one word
I yearn to feel it when I wake
I yearn to feel it 'fore I sleep
When it makes my heart its home
There are no more maybes
When it makes my mind its home
I have direction
When it settles in my soul
I will let you know

A Thousand Times

I've asked you a thousand times before
About the meaning of life
You always gave me the same answer
And I was always partly satisfied
Because it was you talking
Because the answer came from you
But on this one thousand and first time
I am not satisfied with your answer
Even though it is you talking
Even though the answer comes from you
And so I seek a different source
On a path that is terrifying and exhilarating
The only path I've ever known
The only path I'll ever know
And upon thorough examination
The only path I want to walk

Stairs

These stairs are easier to climb today
I've been taking them for eight years straight
I paid in full, I'm fitter now
Maybe the fittest to date
But it's not too late for me
I know something you don't
I'll take this to my grave
Which I'll make for fun's sake
I don't plan on burning in an elevator
Or drowning in a lake
These stairs are easier to climb today
I chose to let them take me higher
Now I'm on top
My elevation correlates to my elation
And I have these stairs to thank

Blind

It seems that often I can only imagine
That we are all the same
In the blink of an eye, my perspective changes
And I see clearly
Our common fragility
Fears
Strengths
Weaknesses
Hopes and
Dreams
I see clearly, but it all feels dream-like
I know it won't last
In the blink of an eye, my perspective changes
And once again, I am blind

Participation

I waited, an inch away from failure
On the rope of success
I opened my closed eyes
To find my feet
Were not shaking
But steady
Life plays tricks
But I was ready
For something greater
A sensical participation
My heart, whole
My love, true
My hair, covered
A once stagnant beauty
Directed forward
I have no intention
Of interfering this time
What will happen, will happen
My savior will forever be participation
In a community
Waiting to be found

Self-Actualization

How many different realities
Can you perceive
At your chosen seat?

Boundaries

The keeper of the queen
Defining boundaries
The caution summoned
Before the need
A filter for present reality
A cure for dry lips, begging for mercy
Proven obsolete by a worker bee
Still, undoubtedly
A wrap to interval-inspired misery
Majestic modesty

Bright

Life was here
It played in all the time
That it was awake
Like a young child
Perpetually in flow state
It spoke up
When nobody else could
Showed the universe
That God was good
This Life was a hero
Gave others hope
By being free
When it was shackled to a burning wall
It smoked up
Saw things beyond imagination
And decided to stay
In fact it was never in its DNA
To give up
So, it didn't give up
It stood up straight
From a state of prostration
We love Life
Makes us dream of bigger things
We're inspired

Like Water

Someone once called me a breath of fresh air
But I want to be like water
Neither here nor there
It just does its thing
Wearing a humility ring

To Be

To think, without jumping
To know, without using
To praise, without tripping
To attribute, without lying
To hope, without soaring
To ask, without forgetting
To find, without falling
To love, without saving

The Space

Where I am, where you will be
Where your essence sets me free
Where the wealth always was
Where my heart chooses to be
Where I'll hear your voice speaking fearlessly
Where my touch will be a challenge to others
You'll find it, effortlessly

Shaken

I sit here
Shaken, but grateful
What just happened?
How did you know?
How did you feel
My impulse starting to fade?
How will you somehow be there
Always?
I'm grateful, to say the least
You're everything and more
But am I supposed to let go of the reins?
Can I really just sit here, shaken
Yet saved?

Recalling Nirvana

Strangers meeting up in a common area
Something happens, but no one knows what
Cupid draws arrow
Misses
Cupid is the distraction
Something happens, but no one knows what
Strangers departing from a common area

One Mind

Fighting the status quo, Goddess exposed
Elusive beauty in Her eye, agreement of one mind
Emergent new ethics, for positivity
An instrumental philosophy
Loving consequences, hearts aligned
A catalyst for equality, one mind

Radio

Torn, but human, still
My eyes shift
To morning dew
All that is left
Is memories of you
Track by track
I move on
Memories intact
Future prevails
Past fails
To wake me
From facing sleep's death
I've won
I've already won
The radio is on
The party has begun

A Fair Fight

I wanted to win
And when I saw I was winning
I wanted a fair fight
I wanted to do it all on my own
And now that I'm this close
I no longer think about justice
I just need you, in my arms
For a fair fight won't make the outcome easier on the others
For if I told the truth
They don't deserve me
And they don't deserve you
I'll stay true
Without losing you

Wisdom

The dearest to the sincere
For they found it all on their own
And they would never sell their soul
Not for peace
Not for things known
They know that they must go with the flow
And go they will
Nomads on the move
Where every home is home

The Child

When the dew quenches the thirst of the patient grass
And the dark sky breaks its fast
A young child wakes
In this room, her eyes barely see
But fear is her friend
She goes back to sleep
She knows not
That the paradise we seek
Lies at her feet

Voices

I hear thoughts
Sometimes they come as yours
I don't know how much space is left
I'm trying to be patient
With a mind, not vacant
I hear thoughts
Sometimes they come as yours

Luck

Within a window of opportunity
Your luck
Is time-sensitive
So claim it or don't claim it
Your luck
Will soon be up

Voodoo

Needle-point
Sharp to the touch
In the mind
In the mind
In the mind
Control in hand
Right arm up
Left hand straight
And out
You are hungry
For something you can't have
I wish I could give it to you
But you thought I had it
And attacked my cold cell
Thinking you'd find it
You found a strand
Of something
You were so sure
It was hair
So you burnt it
Thinking I'd be bald
I woke up with two inches
Of ivory bangs
I thought God did it
I had prayed for longer hair, you see
Who knew your jealousy
Would be a blessing
For my head
I'll remember to leave my cell wide open
So next time you do
Your vindictive voodoo

You'll get a shot at the nucleus
It's time for a change in
Collaborative DNA

Realized

Crawling on the ground floor
Of an ocean of my dreams
Walking, years later
On a path of misery
My feet senselessly scared to make a change
In direction, self-mandated as arbitrary
At last finding flowery fields
That you described to me
Alone
But happy

Everything

To break a bridge of tension
To risk health from wisdom
To have it all
To find that you are not at fault
Yes, I want it all

Innocent

I wrote a thesis, it's written
I stood up for strings
They're hidden
Rhymes and splendid poetry
Have filled my space
I just want to move forward

Fresh face
Comfortable in this skin
I own nothing
I am

My will is strong
Paper retrieved in the air
Feelings kept in my lungs
They're waiting for me
But no, I don't think I'll show

Faux amis
Are here for my convenience
I have time to spend
Give me your hand
And throw the rest away
Intolerance says goodbye
To all it knows
I fought so hard for this
But there was no need to fight
I can see light's signature strokes

The Wire

I promise you
I will never be taken for granted
I will speak up
When the wire is too thin
I will point my finger
At the perpetrator
And that will always
Be enough
I will ask you
To let me go
When you finally realize
God, you are a little clueless
But you won't let go
The tables will do a 180
Without touch
Shattering Newton
And all his foolish followers
Touch is irrelevant
The tables were moving
In the mind of the forgotten
Not in the proposed direction
But in a compromised one
Suggested by two circus tigers
Tamed by a distant wind

Ageless

Each time I forget
You take your shot
But your aim is off
You wonder how
I came to be
How I do what I do
Well, you'd do it too
Wouldn't you
Here's a hint
You'll inevitably miss
I always
Breathe
I have found
The fountain of youth
Why, how, when
Was written when
Time grew fearless
Learning from a benevolent model
I am ageless
Free of weakness
Constantly surrounded
By love and greatness
Love is at a loss
For oxygen
Extinct in the mind of the forgotten

Liquid

You sit, in front of me
I stare, suspending my sense of disbelief
Just last night, you were solid
Your current liquid state has left me in awe
But it's not even your state that alarms me most
You're suddenly part of my flow
Within a consciousness nucleus
I don't think you're aware of the change taking place
In collaborative DNA

Goddess

Here I walk
On a path that led to nowhere once before
But what I'm forging
Is another's space
I'm doing hard work

Granted, things take time
Love erases nothing
Memories are broken
If you don't try to fix them
And they do need fixing

I know what I need to do
I know who I need to see
So I can breathe like I once did
That peace I felt
I swear it's spreading over my face
A blinding visage

Determined, strong, rising with an alarm
That is right in time
But intrinsically wrong
Don't you know
Time doesn't precipitate smoke

Peace

Words of wisdom
Keep it to yourself
Keep it, for your health
For the sake of sanity
For the sake of vanity
Please, keep yourself sane
You know who you are
You know where you want to go
So, be fit
Be the fittest
That flow they speak of?
Consider it

Be True

Be true for you
Do what is meant to be done
Shine when the mirror is in your view
Be true for you

Be true for me
Pray by heart
Continue with the art
Be true for me

Be true for the sake
Of being true

Wonder if they'll ever have a clue

Easy

Flaws in my eyes, flawless in others'
Loud, breaks, shout-outs
Cut to post-bouts
Easy, beautiful, calm
A reference for essays on doubts

Immortality

When the tongue
No longer speaks for the host
When the feet try to shake off their past
In vain, of course
When the fingertips find home
Full of vindication
When home isn't what it used to be
But it's still a place to rest the head
When heart finds health
When health is wealth
When the prize is won
But it's not exactly as was advertised
It's infinitely greater
Self-found mercy from decomposition
Personalized evolution

Reborn

Each moment, I am reborn
I seek the sun, I watch the moon
I gravitate towards the negative
But with the negative comes space
And in that space
I find what I look forward to
Each moment, I am reborn
I seek the sun, I watch the moon

Contentment

Until we land on a path of truth content
Biological needs, grounded in community
Stemming from a reward system
A positive feed
Rivers of dopamine
Once sugar-free

In My Arm

In my arm
I feel it in my arm
It's been there for years, taking my years
I'm being poisoned, with impulsivity
Am I entitled to know truth
Because I know that I said
I would do
Anything for You, this is proof
But what about my dignity, will that ever mend
Or will You be sufficient in the end?
When truth, I can no longer bend

One Day

I wait for that one day
When time creeps up on me
Like a tidal wave
But I do not feel it
Because I am holding hands
With the moon

Castle

Doors are opening
One by one
In a castle fashioned by my mind
That suffering swore to bring right down
Whose progress was maintained by time
Except now I'm seeing my kingdom
Right in front of my eyes
I reflect and prophesize
That this success will come with a perpetual sting
And I'm suspicious of happiness without your ring
But perhaps I was born to be
A queen without a king

Winds

Winds have carved their lines
In my roots
Whistling their views
Leaving permanent grooves
That remind me of my youth
Before I knew winds
When I would seek you
When I could afford to lose my breath
Because I had someone to turn to
But now that I know the truth
I'm relying solely on facts to get me through
I am alone
Being abandoned by everyone and everything
Will not taint my beauty-filled view
Even if I am ungrounded
Over and over by winds
That leave my home in ruins
I am at peace
Because facts are facts
I stand
For truth
It's who I am
Still, with winds, I blow
Granting me resilience needed to grow
I am in submission
To the only one I was ever loyal to
Moving upwards, through Nirvana
Unshaken by erratic winds
Searching for my hidden fruit

Percentages

Driven by disregard
Unfathomable numbers pop up, then disappear
Upon a stage of actors
Until all that remains
Is dust that tells a story of a monologue
A young woman's thoughts
Settle 'neath her own skin
Fixed beliefs, delusions
Colored illness
Yet, the crowd still screams for percentages
For the numbers do not add up
Still
Truth has made Her appearance
This cannot be denied
Just how much of
What She knew
Will manifest
Drives the crowd wild
For, She was available
For such a long time
Her identity dismissed
Her dignity, covered
Her heart, irreparably damaged
Her voice, her pleas
Settled in a mind
She planned to unite with pure creativity
Facilitating thought
About how She must have suffered
As a crowd scrambles for the possibility of forgiveness
While consequences

Dissipate
Leaving a crowd filled with wonder
Without a face to thank

Coincidental

Aches
Thoughts of you conjure a haze of aches
Breaking through consciousness
Making me wake from flavored sleep
Raising my inhibitions that my bones are determined to shake
So that one day
When thoughts of you
Are no longer an issue
And I'm free of this wretched impulsivity
That day, when I'll cease to cave in to manipulations
When I'll know our meeting was only coincidental
I'll be able to claim sobriety from loving you
And I'll have a lifetime to prove to my heart
That it was brave

Glances

These glances stir up feelings
But this time I'm in control
I'm not blinded by an open heart anymore
I dive within, they seek my soul
But they cannot find what they do not know
Protected by fearlessness
Pushed forward by bravery
I am zero
Forever evolving
Persisting in the face of the Absolute

Hypothetical

I made my choice
I used my voice
And maybe the decision was hypothetical
I still made it
So I could respect myself
So that book that they claim lies on my shelf
Would have meaning
I know why I did it
But the reason remains private to everyone else
Making it through the darkest times
Inspired by a go-with-the-flow kind of guy
It just happened
That I lost the dear
That pushed me clear
Out of the way
Of spiritual decay

Last Year

Last year, I fell from Grace
I asked pointless questions
Because I was afraid
I saw Him in your face
And I gave it all up
I'm not to blame
But last year, I did
I fell from Grace

Tyrannical

Tyrannical truth
Feeds me clues
I signed on the line
Where I could lose you
The hidden fee
To which I would never agree
Was the acquisition of endless views
Shots of inhibition
Will not cure
This blindness
Balanced, but tied
There is nothing I can do

The Grid

Fallen, out of the frame
Divinity tries to claim her fame
The reference in an unreal realm
She crosses truth, unwilling to sell
But perspective is crucial
To the hand she's been dealt
Smart plays help her gain
The best kind, straight from hell
Hidden context on a grid
A living constant, invisible

Grace

Grace stands in front of me
Holding on to hope
I don't see anything in her hands
But she's helping me to cope
The lights are dimmed
I don't feel well
I feel I've lost myself
But her eyes are bright, she has faith
She knows something I don't
I don't trust, this pulls me down
In this quick sand, I will drown
But two days later, I see a rope
My hands grab on, I'm suddenly out
No longer in crisis mode, I can breathe once more
I reflect and ask myself
How Grace knew how to help
Did she also hold humility
'Cause my feet have touched the ground

Red Bells

Red bells
I hear red bells
They're sounding out my name
Blue birds
I hear blue birds
But I no longer feel the same
Records
I hear records
Going round and round again
New waves
I hear new waves
They're whispering I'm safe

Claustrophobic

I hear you, I swear
But these walls are closing in on me
And I will not die in this room
I've been patient, I've watched the wave
It's time to try a different way

For How Long

Past a moment's inkling
Once the blood within
Runs dry

For even you
Don't know the will of your blood

The Middle

When the subject in question
Requires addition
A solution exists
Consider the cross
Before, lost
After, found
The cross itself defects
Warnings of distress
Parallel lines prove otherwise
Equal signs, all along
Drawn at any time
Equation, expressed
Before, found
After, lost
Consider the cross

Each Night

A kiss, an embrace
A look that lingers on your face
A whispered promise that takes away the pain
A screen-worthy show that quietly takes place
Am I the last one to realize that we're in a race
Which I forgot to sign up for, in which I cannot pause to wait
There is no time to think
I wake

Inhibition

I pause, I think, I wait
I have a ticket for a plane
The reward for so many smart plays
Soon, I transcend a sphere of shame
One that I've been surviving to break
Falling again
I arrive and find
That all paths are smoothly paved
I walk, then stop
These paths don't lead to where they claim
Yet another trap
For a girl who won't be saved

Established

One part written, two parts established
Temptation bitten, a couple famished
Nirvana in hand, in the arms of comprehension
Two souls braving paths of tension
One part written, two parts established
Temptation hidden, a couple ravished

Natural

I'm working while you sleep
I'll rest when I can't breathe
Which I don't see for me
I prophesize longevity
Instincts kick in, I have what I need
You thought you knew me skin-deep
But I just look
And they're at their knees

Fences

If I forget you
Please remind me when it's cold
All the cold I feel, I feel when you say no

If I forget you
Please remind me when it's warm
All the warmth I feel, I feel when you are home

I don't think I'll forget you
But just in case I do
I wrote you these words
I knew your love was true

Recovery

Drawing once again, emotions in check
Regulation in hand, in the arms of moderation
A pull to prayer, a choice to connect
A confident dawn, filled with acts of remission

Preserved

Free radicals, and there's a solution
Like fresh fruit, effectively frozen
Preserved for a later time
Ready to anti-oxidize, preventing future cancers
Lying in my mind
Sometimes it seems
You're even better there than in person
But I told you
I want good, not better
So, maybe, when you realize
What I've been telling you all along
You'll realize I never gave you up
I met your condition, I'm strong
I've found higher ways
Of staying warm
But will I see you again before your memories thaw?

Lonely

A leaf falling from a tree
Its path in air, unknown
Finally feeling ground
Where it can no longer grow
Just waiting
For the wind to blow

Authenticity

I read, glancing at the givens
A question appears, I conjure responses
I hope for top-grade, I get it
But the mark I saw
Leaves me in reflection

Extrapolation

A question appears, a response is conjured
Facts are facts, and each is honored
A verdict of innocence saves a life
The noose, self-imposed, no longer applies

Free

Heroically holding on
Listening to let go
Wondering if I won't

By the Houses

He's standing there, beside me this time
I recognize him, he's wearing your sadness
I'm willing to listen, to all he has to say
He felt you were his friend, and you led him astray
He knows you provide an oasis for me
So, he's found a new friend
He whispers in my ear
He swears by knowledge I lack
But I don't want to hear it
Baba, please
Come find your shadow
He feels guilty and ashamed
And the feeling's near contagious
He wants change, but does not believe in growth
He won't put in the work, he's looking for a host
And Baba, know this
I have my own shadow
I need light to walk this path
I won't adopt your sorrow

Long-Distance

Something's way overdue
I'm pulling the car over
I'm interrogating you
Get on my side, or we're through
No, tell me the truth
Was it an act, because I was sad
And you knew just what to do
Or are you somehow true
In which case, who's driving who?

Cold

On the floor, a piece of news
Out-stretched arms, but hands refuse
Inner music plays, in tune
Inner music plays, in tune

Paradise

Too close, I lose all hope
From a distance, I still grow

The Method

I assume
You know and I don't

In Honor of My Father

Show me that I'm wrong
I'm open to discussion
I accept that your response
Comes from good intentions

Sometimes, I fear hell
From losing all connection
Still, I'm honest with myself
I will keep reflecting

Belief is not a choice
It is the ultimate blessing
Seeing these words written
I know I'll be forgiven

And I thought I'd lost perspective
But in the blink of an eye
You showed me I could see
I am no longer blind

Legacy

I want to leave a legacy
And have this pen to thank
To look back, in retrospect
And find I did not break
To know my words
Sunk in
That they were worth the fight
That this pen did more than writing
It also saved my life
So I'd get to see the picture
That I always had in mind
And I won't do with average
I'm hungry for success
I pushed all my limits
I almost tasted death
So I could make it back
With wiser words to write
I want to leave a legacy
With a pen that helped unite

Without

Who are you, without
As darkness surrounds
When needs vanish
And desires are in vain
I watch you kneel
Under stars
That glow when you gaze
When darkness promises light
You bow down
Just the same
With or without

The Room

I'm in the dark, cornered
But I've been here before
And I seem to recall that there once was a door
So, I reach out to feel a curtain, instead
When I pull it back, my trembling hands
Aim to steady my knees
For I see my reflection
Staring back, with a smile
Showing two curled up fists
My eyes nowhere in sight

Nihilists Reach Out

When the door is closed
How are we supposed to know?

Changing Lanes

Destination, determined
Formula, facilitated and frozen
Side glances for danger, lurking
Always ensuring that parts were still working
Resisted your hand when I started to fall
I didn't realize then
That I didn't need a net
'Cause it was all for you
Ask me one more time
I always have, always will
I do

2017

It's 2017
But apparently, it's 1984
2+2=5
And nothing is real

Buddhist

Top right, on a slant
Find the space in the chant
Ancient scrolls, paved with peace
A startled audience must retreat
And she leaves
Conceptions, conceived

The Ant

In its purest form
The nature of the ant is to scramble
To curse anything that will slow it down
It does not stop to think of the consequences of being over-worked because it never will be
Its tasks have been delegated from a higher order
And once at the individual ant's level, the tasks are no longer a desire of that ant

Undefined

My heart sinks, quick as sand
When I let go of your hand
Moments pass, time collects
My hopes and dreams, with a promise
To return the goodness of my secret
Undefined-fold

Sugar-Coat

Do not say sugar-coat
For that is counter to your cause
We enjoy the truth, unaltered
We were never at a loss
May the potential for plasticity
Stretch towards
Our hearts
Whose patience cannot be measured
They knew us from the start

Equals

To find hope, to seize it from the clutches of the night
To let go, of letting go
For the noble goal of moving forwards

Directions

You are, in fact, mistaken
Let that sink in
Whatever you believe
There is a better explanation
How else could you find the courage
To choose
New directions?

Energy

The kinetic
The potential for physical disclosure
With friction in the works
And knowledge at disposal
Communication that lasts
Until it's over
With various imprints of doing
So many voids to choose from

Nirvana

A view that exists to see
What otherwise would not be
Particles huddled at the start
A motion picture in the dark
Strange creatures of light
Distracting figures, falling to be seen
Music that plays silently
Beckoning hands, asking for a chance
Thorny fruit, though that may be a stretch
A lit stage, a singing chef
A welcome to the morning, an advertisement
Slowly fading to black
A feeling I cannot perceive
An unsightly regurgitation of speech
A step-by-step lesson on how to breathe
And still, I seek
But the message remains
Yourself, be
As you please, do
I could never have planned for You

Physics

A profound explanation
For what cannot be
Nihilism's proudest discovery
The go-to tool for the creative being
When you say, be
I say, how
You say, I'm not leaving
Enter chemistry

Puzzle Pieces

Anxious, but there is no need
Our turns will soon arrive
We will be handled and examined
Used, or thrown aside
There are stories of those who have gone missing
Their fates and ours, untied
They have been freed
Our destiny, denied

One

I dream of change
Outside of this domain
I am only complete
When we meet
Still of change, I dream
I know where I will be

I Swear by Stars

I swear by stars
That their distance will take me far

Death

An agreed-upon shift in consciousness
But I want to go in peace
If what I perceive
Pertains not to reality
What does it mean for my scale of certainty
If the credibility of the ruling judge is at stake
What remains?

How can trust be found
If I am bound to a brain
That requires tolerance of the absurd
Which breaks down each uttered word
Cross-referencing all indexical terms
Creating volumes of truth that no one has heard

My destination lies in a realm, real
And the path I walk is one of transparency
I seek a well-intentioned end, through a solution-perspective lens
I navigate consciousness, making use of an algorithm, unfixed
I live in my moment, letting be what is
Denying a deal with life
I will not be indebted to death

Dancing Down the Stairs

Apprehensive, I take my first step
Down, I go
Fast, then slow
As my hands find the railing
I pause, midway
If I have forgotten something
Now is the time to return
But I'd rather move forward
I dance down the stairs
As my left foot touches the ground
I am grateful for my right
I have arrived safely
And I am reminded of the preciousness of life

The Camel

You are always prepared, always
You're a fighter, sure
But will you ever know flight
You may never stress, because you're always doing your best
But will you ever be free

Your instincts are to reserve
With the material world, you are concerned
This life is all you know, the only thing in your sight
You don't stop to wonder about the sky
That
Is the domain of dreaming birds

Hussein

I wanted to be there
With him, on the field
Didn't think I was brave
I committed to giving him
All
Of me

Wanted to be on his side
Though we were different times
To stand by his cause
Though it is not me to take sides

Felt I owed it to him
For not shedding tears
Every year
For not knowing him better, for not putting in the effort
For not wanting to

When I lost him, so strange, I was in such pain

I wanted to be there
With him, on the field
I am brave
My love will not go to waste

Veto

You can call me names
And curse my image
Play mind games
Lie about my religion
But I stood up for you
So you could have a seat
And let everyone at the table
Hear you speak
But we'll have to agree I did all of the work
And what you do determines your worth
Did you really think I would give power to crazy?

Evil

Evil knows no bounds
Existing to be found
And You are far removed
But I have known truth

For that, I have a chance

To know that evil has its place
I fight just to stay the same
Who am I to ask for change?

I just want to stay true
And if to believe in
Is to give power to
It will not help to believe
In someone so far removed

Hell

Hell is to know you can't go back
To have remorse, true
To know there's nothing you can do

To be forgiven by the Absolute
To find it not to be of use

To master the art of an infallible excuse
To learn that it won't do

To find the highest heaven because you knew

When

The most important and simultaneously fruitless endeavor is to ask when
What brings you in
Where makes you believe
How keeps you reflecting
Who humbles you
But
When defines you
And since it is impossible to know when until it arrives, when changes you

In Vain

Perhaps I was created in vain
What an idea

After all this pain
What an idea

After all that coordinated hate
What an idea

If I were created in vain
In vain, I will create

Glass

You are a mirror for others
So far, you have this fate
Reflecting each and every trait

At you, they gaze in wonder
By you, themselves, they praise
You are a reliable reference
To which they adjust their face

You see them at their best and worst
What you see, you display

You've only known yourself through others
And you're vulnerable to cracks
But you just might reincarnate
You have the life of glass

God-Willing

God-willing, my dear

These words that I hear
Seem so sincere
That I almost believe
What is presented to me
In the midst of despair
And then I remember
Why I am here
And not there
God-willing, I dared

Shapes

A cloud of color rising with the heat
Sweat dripping down flushed cheeks
Open expressions, conveyed on blank sheets
Linked hands, variable vertices
Curved lines, changing shapes
Moments away from Grace

Imagine

I still bear
The memories you made
Caught my gaze and screamed action

Swore that I'd hurt you
And that I knew what to do
If I had an ounce of compassion

Opened my hand
And placed a knife
I was devastated

I survived to analyze
The dreaded
How on earth could I
And found that I could not

What happened
Happened in my mind
And you asked me to imagine

Christian

When the hour comes
I am a Christian in church

Wearing modest clothes
My speech, reserved
I do not bite my tongue
For you could say no wrong

By your wise words
I sit, listening

When the hour comes
I am a Christian in church

Hell Is for Hypocrites

Hell is for hypocrites, not those who disbelieve
Disbelievers cannot be faulted
For not submitting entirely
To a will that does not bend

Take me, for instance
I did my best to see
But I would not lie
To a God that was so clear
In that which was accepted

I know He's there
His signs are loud
In this sense, I do not doubt

I took the time to understand
The path of brotherly love
But I won't kneel if I don't mean it
To a God that knows my heart

I don't lie to Him
I know I never could
Because the last thing I will be
Is a hypocrite

The Problem with Maybe

Is it nobler to say maybe?
I doubt this very much
I believe in belief
Maybe is a crutch

Don't you see?
With your maybe
The path you seek
Is just out of reach

Hate

When I find it foreign
My mind drifts
No matter how many times I refocus
My attention slips
And that is the nature of human experience

Love has a grand reputation
But it has limits
Hate is refocused, like elusive attention

But hate has a flaw
That should be noted
It codes
For neutralization

When love resists
Hate has loving consequences

In the face of hate, love tolerates
The cycle of violence ends
Love
Is all that is left

Love

I lead the cavemen
Out of their cave
It is easier to spot a group
From the moon, where you stay
This is my SOS
But I will not be saved
I am the reference
You are the frame

Fresh

Window, in view
I'm forgetting about you
I'm tailoring my speech
To words
That will not re-open old wounds
I feel fresh
Forgetting about you
Window, in view

Vision

I met him
And released the power of his
Sight
Everywhere I went
I had a vision
He was the prize
I single-handedly saved
The devil
And I don't know why I ever
Expressed compassion for anything
Other than
Light

Original Creation Dictation

They're not real
They are works of art
Come to life
Original creation dictation
Fixed about a frame
Existing to engage my attention

Some smile
Some have permanent frowns
Others lend a hand
And I'm sure I was mistaken before

But what is art without movement and light

The aesthetic effect is real
But they are not
They are simply works of art
Come to life
And I
Hold the brush

Actress

A screenplay, beautifully written
I say my lines as you've outlined
Under your direction
With intervals of hesitation
Natural silences, destined for interpretation
Scenes that sell

Tears fall down my cheeks
The audience is relieved
Their dollars have not been wasted

The curtains close
We are alone

Didn't I tell you that I was an actress

Earth

Sometimes
Earth speaks wisdom, too
But eyes are to remain open
If heart is to stay closed

Leaving the Circle

I take
The throne
I sit down
Feel the weight of the crown
Kneel forwards
And look out at the crowd

One by one
I see a standing group
Fall to the ground
As if a forest of trees is prostrating

I
Do not move

I do not browse
Through the faces
I've seen them all before

The sound of your voice
Rings in my ear
As you place your hand on mine

It's time, my dear

Willing

Your words were
The contingency plan for us
My soul
Was the contingency plan for them
Every breath, every glance
You made sure I knew
That I will always be loved by you
At the very least
Everything would be okay
At the most
An extension to an infinite heaven

I Did Not Choose

I did not choose
But the promise of heaven was empty without you

I've let you go
Too many times to be sure
I gave you every reason to leave
God knows I couldn't bear to smile for too long

But you stay

In a box, I put your message away
All other memories, I continue to erase
Destroyed evidence of better days

Even asked God to be my witness
By God, I did not choose you over Him
Then I let go of Him too
For what kind of heaven does not feature you

But you persevere
On me, you don't give up
These tears still fall
To your unconditional love

I make sure to stay away from the box
I don't want to fuel the storm

God keeps showing me dreams
That I do not care to see
And I know it's because
He doesn't want to lose me

Still, the choice remains mine
And I've decided to put it on hold
I found the flow of which you spoke
And I'm letting it carry me home

And I did not choose
But the promise of heaven was empty without you

Sacred

An infinite line of thoughts
Waiting to be expressed

I
Could
Get
Lost

Lost in the words
Lost in the language

Truth
Is the prize
But I resist distraction
For Truth does not compare to You

An infinite line of thoughts
Waiting to be expressed

But You are
Sacred

CPSIA information can be obtained
at www.ICGtesting.com
Printed in the USA
LVHW081945060420
652380LV00016B/246

9 781643 788197